The Great Divorce Study Guide

A Bible Study on the
The Great Divorce by C.S. Lewis

By Alan Vermilye

"If we insist on keeping Hell (or even earth) we shall not see Heaven: if we accept Heaven we shall not be able to retain even the smallest and most intimate souvenirs of Hell." *The Great Divorce*

The Great Divorce Study Guide
A Bible Study on The Great Divorce by C.S. Lewis

Copyright © 2017 Alan Vermilye
Brown Chair Books

ISBN-13: 978-1547067442

To learn more about this Bible study, to order additional copies, or to download the answer guide, visit **www.BrownChairBooks.com**.

Version 1

ACKNOWLEDGMENTS

I would like to thank C.S. Lewis for writing such a fun book to both read and then to create a Bible study for! I would also like to thank my family for supporting me in writing these studies and for those who participated in my teaching of this course…especially my teenage daughter, Maddie, who held her own in a class full of adults.

TABLE OF CONTENTS

INTRODUCTION

What is the most desirable place you can think of to take a vacation? Perhaps it is a place that you have been before or someplace you dream of going. How would you respond if, once you arrived, you were invited to stay on this vacation forever? However, in order to stay, you must leave your old life behind. You cannot go back and say goodbye or set your affairs in order. You either must commit at that moment or return to your previous life.

How hard would it be for you to leave behind the life you are now living? It might be an easy decision for some and much more difficult for others.

In *The Great Divorce* by C.S. Lewis, damned spirits are given a vacation or a "holiday" away from Hell to visit Heaven, where they are invited to stay forever. There, they are persuaded by people they formally knew, relatives and friends, to come with them up the mountain to enjoy the bliss of Heaven. But they can only do so by leaving behind what is keeping them in Hell and accepting the love of God.

The answer seems obvious, right? Yet what we'll find is that it's not the choice to sin that binds people to Hell but rather the choice not to repent. We must let go, step out into the light, and embrace the better life that God has planned for us. That's the most confining part about sin—to admit you're in the wrong.

Lewis tells us not to take this story literally, nor does he suppose that eternity really is the way he presents it in the book. The fact is, Hell is final. Scripture records no opportunities offered after death to enter Heaven. On the title page of your book by Lewis, there is a telling quote from George MacDonald: "No, there is no escape. There is no heaven with a little of hell in it—no plan to retain this or that of the devil in our hearts or our pockets. Out Satan must go, every hair and feather."

In this story, Lewis quite vividly illustrates for us that we are all soul searching and our efforts either move us toward or away from God. It's a progression away from our own idea of what we think is best for us toward the humility required to embrace God's best for our lives. It can be painful to leave our old life behind, but with each step, it gets a little easier, and any pain will be nothing compared to the joy we will experience in Heaven.

I thoroughly enjoyed putting together this Bible study. As with all my studies, I write them for the small groups that I facilitate at my own church. Not only does it help better refine the study but I also learn from each class member as they share their interpretation of what they read. I'm eternally grateful for their participation and input on the study.

As for my normal disclaimer, I'm not a biblical or Lewis scholar nor do I consider this study guide the most comprehensive work available on the book. However, it has helped me and others in my class come to a better understanding of Lewis's great classic. I hope it does the same for you as well.

BOOK SUMMARY

Although this summary does not include every detail of the book, it does provide an overview of the story. For that reason, if, like a great movie, you do not want the end spoiled, I encourage you to skip this summary and move on to reading the book.

The plot for *The Great Divorce* in actually fairly straightforward. By all accounts, Lewis appears to be the protagonist and narrator guiding us through a series of events beginning with his waiting in a long line for a magical bus ride in a dismally uncomforting grey town—which is in fact Hell or Purgatory.

His companions in line are argumentative, combative, and generally disagreeable and of differing economic and educational backgrounds. These unpleasant and contentious souls are traveling on refrigerium, or holiday, where they're allowed to visit other places outside of Hell. Most visit Earth, while a few others make this bus trip to the outer banks of Heaven.

As they board and the bus leaves the ground, Lewis begins conversing with others aboard about the grey town—this seedy and empty city that stretches on forever and where time seems to be paused. He learns that evening never advances to night; it's dreary, dull, dirty, and bleak, and it's always raining. It is a place, for all its vastness, that seems insubstantial with very few people milling around.

In addition to the grey town being a somber, desolate place, its quarreling inhabitants are constantly spreading throughout the town so as to be as far away from each other as possible. They cannot find any good with each other that would draw them together. As a result, there is no community, since there is no need to rely on one another. Some, after being there for centuries, have actually moved lightyears away from the bus stop, which prevents them from making the long journey back.

The residents in the grey town get everything they want, but not of great quality, by simply imagining it. They can think structures, homes, and other things into existence, but nothing is able to meet their needs in a substantive way. For example, if one desires a house, it is there, but it will not keep out the rain or danger. For this reason, they venture off to build a new house, and the town continues to spread.

The bus flies for hours through darkness until it approaches a beautiful countryside. As the travelers exit the bus, some become overwhelmed and retreat back to the safety of the bus, while others, braver, huddle together and press forward into the vast, beautiful unknown.

The landscape, including the grass, flowers, mountains, etc., is all beautiful in appearance, but it is also solid and heavy so that the blades of grass are as sharp and hard as diamonds and cause terrible pain just to walk on. Even a single leaf is too heavy to lift. The light and coolness remind Lewis of a summer morning, and the "fresh stillness" and the "singing of a lark" are in stark contrast to what he experienced in the grey town.

Soon they are approached by the resident Spirits of Heaven, who are filled with a great light; they are very grand and seemingly ageless. Some are naked, some are robed, and others have beards, but all are muscular with smooth flesh, and the earth shakes underneath their feet as they are solid, not transparent like the Ghosts from the grey town.

The Spirits are relatives and friends the Ghosts formerly knew on earth. They encourage the Ghosts to abandon the grey town and come with them up the mountain to enjoy the bliss of Heaven. Each Spirit is gentle but also direct in helping the Ghosts recognize their sin and their need for redemption. The Ghosts are assured that as they leave behind their pride, hatred, and unbelief and progress toward the mountain with the Spirits, it will get easier as they will begin to feel more solid.

Unfortunately, the majority of the Ghosts refuse to acknowledge their sin and instead seek to justify themselves. They would rather return to the grey town retaining their own sovereignty than submit themselves to God and agree with His evaluation of them.

After witnessing a variety of conversations between Ghosts and Spirits, Lewis realizes that each Ghost represents a character study of human nature and the struggle with sin. In fact, many of their sins are not what we might consider evil or diabolical, yet they still are unable to enter Heaven. This leaves Lewis confused, miserable, and somewhat fearful.

At last, he is approached by his guiding Spirit, who is none other than author, poet, and Christian minister George MacDonald. MacDonald answers Lewis's most pressing questions regarding the fate of the Ghosts he finds himself with, including, "Do any of them stay? Can they stay? Is any real choice offered to them? How do they come to be here?"

According to MacDonald, while it is possible for a soul to choose to leave Hell and enter Heaven, doing so implies repenting of their sin and embracing ultimate and unceasing joy itself. For those souls who decide to stay, they never would have been in Hell but rather Purgatory. They will soon discover that their worst pain has been used by God for redemptive purposes to prepare them to be with Him in eternity. The converse is also true for those who choose Earth over Heaven; they will miss out on the joys of serving a living God and actually find that Hell is not that much different from the life they led on Earth: joyless, friendless, and uncomfortable.

As to why the Spirits don't travel to the grey town to rescue its ghostly inhabitants, Lewis discovers that both the town and the Ghosts are minuscule to the point of being invisible compared with the immensity of heaven. Even if they wanted to, the Spirits' size and goodness would prevent them from ever entering Hell.

In the end, MacDonald finally confirms to Lewis that he is dreaming. As the sun begins to rise in Lewis's dream, he becomes both surprised and terrified of remaining a Ghost in the advent of full daybreak in Heaven, comparing the experience to having large blocks of light falling on him. At this point, he awakens to books falling on his head.

Through his journey, Lewis is convinced of the goodness and mercy of God as well as his own need and the urgency for redemption.

Character Summary

LEWIS / PROTAGONIST / NARRATOR

The story is written in the first person with the narrator never being identified by name, but inferences point to it being C.S. Lewis. His character is both a learned man and drawn to literary giants like George MacDonald, whose writings had an impact on Lewis's life. For this reason, throughout the study guide we will refer to the narrator as Lewis.

In the story, Lewis is primarily an observer of the other Ghosts and their discussions with the Spirit Guides. It is through these discourses that he comes to understand the insidious nature of sin and the grip it has on human nature and our seeming inability to let it go—even when given the opportunity for infinite joy.

THE SPIRIT GUIDES

The Spirit Guides are residents of Heaven who have been glorified after death through their trust and faith in Jesus Christ. Each Spirit approaches a Ghost he or she had a relationship with during their earthly life. They encourage the Ghosts to abandon the grey town and to come up with them to the mountain to enjoy the bliss of Heaven. The Spirits are gentle but also direct in helping the Ghosts recognize their sin and need for redemption. The majority of the Ghosts view the Spirits as being antagonistic and thereby refuse their offer and abandon Heaven, not wanting to confront their sin.

GEORGE MACDONALD

Lewis's guiding spirit is none other than author, poet, and Christian minister George MacDonald, whose works include *Phantastes, The Princess and the Goblin,* and *At the Back of the North Wind.* McDonald's work had a profound influence on Lewis during his earthly life and, in this story, serves as a father figure and mentor type in the afterlife helping Lewis to understand the ways of Heaven.

THE TOUSEL-HAIRED POET

The tousle-haired poet feels unappreciated by most everyone he meets. His distaste for capitalism drives him to communism and eventually to becoming a conscientious objector due to his disdain for war. He has an excessive desire for attention and need for respect from others that leaves him feeling like the victim when he does not receive any. His self-pity is so strong that he ended his life by throwing himself under a train, not desiring to live in a world that was against him.

IKEY (THE INTELLIGENT GHOST)

The Intelligent Ghost is a thriving entrepreneur. He does not believe the problem in the grey town is that people quarrel but rather that they have no needs. His solution is to travel to Heaven and bring back, or steal, "some real commodities," or saleable goods, that would generate demand. This foolish attempt to profit from Heaven leaves him battered and bruised, unable to lift any solid apples to take back with him.

FAT GHOST (WITH GAITERS)

The Fat Ghost believes the old theology of Hell and judgment are outdated superstitions and what the inhabitants of the town really need is spirituality unencumbered by any materialism and matter. In fact, he is unaware that the grey town he has inhabited is Hell until the Spirit he encounters reveals him as an apostate living in Hell. His sin is of the intellect since he has embraced liberal theology and rejected the resurrection of Christ for success and position within the church.

THE BIG GHOST

This man is astonished and outraged to find Len, the Guiding Spirit he encounters, enjoying life in Heaven. He recognizes Len only as an earthly murderer and cannot understand why Len is here in Heaven and he himself is in the grey town since he believes he was a much better man on Earth. Len does his best to persuade the Big Ghost to acknowledge his faults, but he wants no part of a Heaven that allows murderers to become citizens.

THE HARD-BITTEN GHOST

During his earthly life, this man traveled much of the world, building only a cynical view of what he experiences. He is suspicious, does not trust anyone, and develops conspiracies about most everything, including Heaven and Hell. He says that he knows all about Heaven and that it's the same old lie he's heard all his life.

THE WELL-DRESSED GHOST

During both her earthly life and in the afterlife, this woman's vanity drives her to become completely self-absorbed, if not ashamed, and unable to see anyone but herself. In an attempt to shake her from this preoccupation with self, the attending Spirit calls a herd of unicorns to create some sort of diversion that would draw her mind away from herself and to God.

THE SCIENTIST GHOST

MacDonald tells Lewis of this ghost whose scientific research consumed his life; he eventually died and made it to the outskirts of Heaven. He decided not to continue on to the mountains because there was nothing in Heaven left to prove, no question that he could provide an answer for. He could not overcome his disappointment and simply accept God as "a little child and [enter] into joy."

THE GRUMBLING GHOST

This female ghost has allowed occasional complaining and grumbling to become full-fledged sin that has consumed her life. MacDonald assures Lewis, who thinks she's just a silly old woman who has gotten into a bad habit, that if there's a spark of the woman left, she can be saved.

THE SENSUAL GHOST

This ghost is completely self-consumed with her appearance, believing she can seduce the Spirits with her body and completely unaware that her body is no longer substantial or enticing.

THE FAMOUS ARTIST GHOST

The Artist Ghost was quite famous on Earth and had begun painting as a means to tell about the light, but over time he lost that desire and just painted for painting sake. He now finds himself interested only in painting God's creation but not actually interested in God Himself. He is encouraged by his Spirit Guide to drink from a fountain that will cause him to forget all of his earthly works and create an appreciation of all work without false modesty or pride.

THE OVERBEARING WIFE GHOST

This ghost is hypocritical, depressing, critical, and self-centered. She is extremely controlling of her husband, Robert, and treats him more like her property, having nagged him to death in their earthly life. Her self-image rests solely on the actions of others—specifically that of her husband.

THE MOTHERLY GHOST

Disappointed to be greeted in Heaven by her brother, Reginald, this Motherly Ghost had made an idol of her love for her son, Michael. Her desire to see her son is stronger than her desire for God and is ultimately what prevents her from growing solid and continuing into Heaven.

THE OILY GHOST AND HIS LIZARD

This Ghost is described as a "dark and oily" smoke with a little red lizard sitting on its shoulder that is constantly touching its tail and whispering in the Ghost's ear. The lizard is the embodiment of some type of lust. The Ghost thinks he can keep it under control, at least in the polite company of Heaven, but he cannot. The Spirit offers to kill the lizard but says he is only free to do so with the Ghost's consent.

SARAH SMITH

MacDonald refers to Sarah Smith as "one of the great ones." She's beautiful, warm, loving, and seemingly capable of infinite kindness. In the afterlife, Sarah has a large "family" because on Earth, she was kind and gracious to many different people, even people whom she barely knew. On Earth, Sarah and the dwarf, whose name is Frank, were married, and she preceded him in death. Although not famous on Earth, in Heaven, Sarah is a saint. Lewis picks the name Sarah Smith for this very reason—to emphasize her plainness.

FRANK THE DWARF GHOST AND THE TRAGEDIAN

Frank has a "divided nature" split between two figures, the Dwarf and the Tragedian—an old-school, melodramatic actor who specializes in tragic roles. The real Frank is the "Dwarf," who becomes less and less himself the more he feeds his persona or alter ego, the Tragedian, who projects the dwarf's need to be pitied and apologized to.

MacDonald elaborates on other types of Ghosts that come near to Heaven but do not stay:

TEACHING GHOSTS

The most common was the type that wanted to tell, teach, or lecture the Celestials on Hell.

TUB-THUMPING GHOSTS

A tub-thumper is a noisy, violent, or ranting public speaker—the radical revolutionaries demanding that the Spirits rise up and free themselves from "happiness," tear down the mountains, and "seize Heaven for their own."

PLANNING GHOSTS

These Ghosts encouraged the Spirits to dam the river, kill the animals, and pave the horrible grass with nice smooth asphalt.

MATERIALIST GHOSTS

These Ghosts informed Spirits that there is no life after death and that everything is a hallucination.

BOGIE GHOST

These Ghosts realize they have deteriorated into mere shadows and have now taken up the traditional ghostly role of scaring whomever they can.

COURSE NOTES AND STUDY FORMAT

HOW TO USE THIS GUIDE

The Great Divorce consists of fourteen chapters and can easily be read in an afternoon. This study guide can be used for individual study or as a group study meeting weekly to discuss each chapter.

STUDYING

Each week you will read select chapters, which are approximately five to eight pages each. Each chapter is fairly short and easily digested with the exception of a few. As you read, make notes in your book and underline or highlight sections that interest you. As you work through each session, make note of any other questions you have in the Notes section at the end of each study. The answers to each question can be found at www.BrownChairBooks.com. However, do not cheat yourself. Work through each session prior to viewing the answers.

GROUP FORMAT

For group formats, the study works well over an eight-week period. The first week is an introduction week to hand out study guides (if purchased by the church), read through the introduction and character sketches, and set a plan and schedule for the remaining seven weeks. You might also have those who have previously read the book share their thoughts and experiences.

This study can certainly be used by Sunday school classes, but recognize that Sunday morning time in many churches is relatively short. Thus, the study lends itself very well to midweek times at the church or in the homes of members. Session length is variable.

Ideally, you should allow at least 90 minutes per session. For longer sessions, take a quick refreshment break in the middle.

As a group leader, your role will be to facilitate the group sessions using the study guide and the answers found at www.BrownChairBooks.com. Recognize that you are the facilitator. You are not the answer person; you are not the authority; you are not the judge to decide if responses are right or wrong. You are simply the person who tries to keep the discussion on track and in the timeframe allowed while keeping everyone involved, heard, and respected.

LEARNING ENVIRONMENT

The following are some suggestions for shaping the learning environment for group sessions that help manage time, participation, and confidentiality.

- Ask the Holy Spirit for help as you prepare for the study. Pray for discernment for each member of the group, including yourself.
- Before each session, familiarize yourself with the questions and answers as it may have been several days since you completed the session. Consider reading the weekly chapters again.
- Be prepared to adjust the session as group members interact and questions arise. Allow for the Holy Spirit to move in and through the material, the group members, and yourself.
- Arrange the meeting space to enhance the learning process. Group members should be seated around a table or in a circle so that they can all see one another. Moveable chairs are best.
- Download the quick Bible reference handout at www.BrownChairBooks.com, and distribute it at the beginning of class to save time looking up Scripture.
- If using Bibles, bring extras for those who forget to bring one or for those who might not have one. (If someone is reading aloud, you might ask the person to identify from which Bible translation he or she is reading.)
- If your teaching style includes recording responses from participants or writing questions or quotations for discussion on a board, you may want access to a whiteboard or an easel.
- Agree on the class schedule and times. In order to maintain continuity, it would be best if your class meets for eight consecutive weeks.

- The suggested session time is 90 minutes. Because each chapter can lead to substantial discussion, you may need to make choices about what you will cover, or you may choose to extend your group sessions to allow more time for discussion.

- Create a climate where it is safe to share. Encourage group members to participate as they feel comfortable. Remember that some will be eager to give answers or offer commentary, while others will need time to process and think.

- If you notice that some participants are hesitant to enter the conversation, ask if they have thoughts to share. Give everyone an opportunity to talk, but keep the conversation moving. Intervene when necessary to prevent a few individuals from dominating the discussion.

- If no one answers at first during a discussion, do not be afraid of silence. Count silently to ten, and then say, "Would anyone like to go first?" If no one responds, provide your own answer and ask for reactions. If you limit your sharing to a surface level, others will follow suit. Keep in mind that if your group is new, cohesion might take a couple of weeks to form. If group members do not share at first, give them time.

- Encourage multiple answers or responses before moving on.

- Ask "Why?" or "Why do you believe that?" or "Can you say more about that?" to draw out greater depth from a response.

- Affirm others' responses with comments such as "Great" or "Thanks" or "Good insight"—especially if this is the first time someone has spoken during the group session.

- Monitor your own contributions. If you are doing most of the talking, back off so that you do not train the group to listen rather than speak.

- Honor the designated time window. Begin on time. If a session runs longer than expected, get consensus from the group before continuing.

- Involve participants in various aspects of the session, such as offering prayer and reading Scripture.

- Because some questions call for sharing personal experiences, confidentiality is essential. Remind group members at each session of the importance of confidentiality and of not passing along stories that have been shared in the group.

SUGGESTED SESSION OUTLINE

Based on the amount of reading each week, we suggest that you follow the study outline below over an eight-week period, but you are by no means locked in to this format. The key is group interest and involvement, not the calendar.

Date	Time	Session	Chapters
		Week 1	Introduction
		Week 2	Preface, Chapters 1 and 2
		Week 3	Chapters 3 and 4
		Week 4	Chapters 5 and 6
		Week 5	Chapters 7 and 8
		Week 6	Chapter 9
		Week 7	Chapters 10 and 11
		Week 8	Chapters 12, 13, and 14

PREFACE

Summary

In the opening preface of the book, Lewis elaborates on what we all should know—that you cannot have both Heaven and Hell at the same time. It's either one or the other. This sounds obvious, right? But often we live our lives contrary to that belief by clinging to those worldly vices and values that have no place in the Christian life, much less Heaven. According to Lewis, "Evil can be undone, but it cannot 'develop' into good." The fact is, we must wholly reject evil for Heaven to be fully embraced.

> *If we insist on keeping Hell (or even Earth) we shall not see Heaven: if we accept Heaven we shall not be able to retain even the smallest and most intimate souvenirs of Hell.*

Discussion Questions

William Blake wrote *The Marriage of Heaven and Hell* between 1790 and 1793. In this book, he tells us that good and evil aren't really what we think they are. They're just different kinds of energies, and both are needed to keep the world going. The Bible and other religious texts, he says, have been responsible for a lot of the misinformation we've been given. He claims that two types of people exist: the "energetic creators," or devils from Hell, and the "rational organizers," or angels from heaven, of which he claims both are necessary to life.

1. Why do you think humanity is constantly searching for opportunities to blur the lines between good and evil? Why is this dangerous ground to tread?

2. What attempts do you see in today's culture of trying to "marry" Heaven and Hell, and how do you think this dysfunctional marriage has changed culture today?

3. Read Isaiah 5:20. What did Isaiah say to warn the nation of Israel that they were in rebellion against God? What specifically were they doing? Do you think God's standards have changed since the time of Isaiah? Why or why not?

4. Lewis disagreed with Blake. In his view, all good comes from God, nothing good comes from Hell, and there can be no legitimate marriage of the two. Read Matthew 5:29–30. On the journey to Heaven, which "luggage" cannot be carried along and why might we have to leave our "right hand" and "right eye" behind?

5. Explain what Lewis meant by "Evil can be undone, but it cannot 'develop' into good." According to Romans 12:21, how is evil overcome?

6. What does Lewis say will happen if we insist on keeping Hell? If we accept Heaven, what will we not be able to keep? If we accept Heaven, what will we find?

7. Why does Lewis put in his "disclaimer" at the conclusion of the Preface?

PREFACE DISCUSSION NOTES:

CHAPTER 1:
THE NATURE OF HELL

As the story begins, Lewis, also our narrator, finds himself waiting in a long line for a magical bus ride in a dismally uncomforting grey town. His companions in line are argumentative, combative, and generally disagreeable and of differing economic and educational backgrounds. As the story progresses we learn that these characters are damned souls on vacation, and that the grey town is Purgatory for some and the outskirts of Hell for others.

Why on earth they insist on coming I can't imagine. They won't like it at all when we get there, and they'd really be much more comfortable at home.

Discussion Questions

1. Describe in detail the mood, atmosphere, images, and depictions of the grey town. Do you find Lewis's depiction of Hell or Purgatory "accurate"?

2. Although the grey town is revealed within the contexts of the story to be the outer limits of Hell, or Purgatory for those who will eventually reach Heaven, the reader is to consider this an imaginative representation of Hell rather than an accurate, biblical representation of the real Hell. Using the following Bible passages, describe the nature of Hell. In your own words, how would you describe Hell to a friend?

    a) Revelation 14:10–11 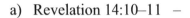 –

    b) 2 Thessalonians 1:9 –

    c) Revelation 21:8 –

    d) Matthew 25:41 –

    e) Mark 9:44–49 –

    f) Revelation 20:10 –

    g) Matthew 13:41–42 –

    h) Matthew 3:12 –

    i) Daniel 12:2 –

    j) Luke 16:23–24 –

3. The souls that Lewis encounters while waiting for and getting on the bus seem to represent various forms of sin in what used to be called the capital sins or what is commonly referred to as the seven deadly sins. Associate the different personalities he encounters in line and on the bus with the appropriate sin below.

    a) Envy – the desire to have an item, an experience, or feeling that someone else possesses

b) Gluttony – an excessive, ongoing consumption of food or drink

c) Greed – an excessive pursuit of material possessions

d) Lust – an uncontrollable passion or longing, especially for sexual desires

e) Vanity or Pride – excessive view of one's self without regard to others

f) Sloth – excessive laziness or the failure to act and utilize one's talents

g) Wrath or Anger – uncontrollable feelings of anger and hate toward another person

4. As people continue to leave the bus line, what principle is Lewis trying to establish regarding a town in which any real life is absent yet there is little desire to move beyond it?

5. The souls complain about the bus driver, saying, "Why can't he behave naturally?" Read 1 Corinthians 2:14. Why do unbelievers have difficulty relating to or understanding a believer's joy?

6. The tousle-haired poet cannot imagine why the other souls would insist on coming on the bus and concludes that they would be much more comfortable at home. What parallel is there to our comfort and how we deal with sin? Read 1 John 1:8 and Romans 12:9. How do we break free of that sin comfort zone?

7. What do you think of Lewis's idea that there will be fish and chips and movies and advertising in Hell?

CHAPTER 1 DISCUSSION NOTES:

CHAPTER 2: A BUS RIDE INTO HEAVEN

As the bus is en route to an unknown, but presumably better, destination, we learn a little bit more about the grey town as well as the passengers on the bus. It is in this setting that we learn that not all of the passengers are going to Heaven for the right reasons but rather to get something for themselves.

> *The trouble is they have no Needs. You get everything you want*
> *(not very good quality, of course) by just imagining it.*

Discussion Questions

1. Describe the tousle-haired poet. What was this young man's sin? What do you think he expects to find or receive once he gets to Heaven?

2. Read John 5:5–9. Why do you think Jesus asked the invalid of 38 years if he really wanted to be healed? Do you think some people do not want to be healed and would rather remain a victim of their circumstances? If so, why?

3. According to Hebrews 12:1, what would Paul say to someone who has claimed the victim mentality and let self-pity creep into their life?

4. Next we are introduced to the Intelligent Ghost. What more do we learn about the grey town from him? What correlation does the man draw to the length of time people have been there and their chances of making it to the bus stop?

5. On a scale of 1 to 10, how would you rate the need for community in your life (neighbors, church, local stores, school, etc.)? Why would you choose that rating? Have you seen this need fade due to technology, the busy pace of life, or something else?

6. What did the Intelligent Ghost believe his job was? Where is the flaw in his plan?

7. According to the Intelligent Ghost, why do the residents of Hell build "unreal" houses that do not keep out the rain or danger? Read Matthew 19:16–22. Just like the residents of Hell, what did the rich young ruler believe provided him a "feeling of safety"? What false sense of security do we substitute for Jesus today that we believe provides us with a "feeling of safety"?

8. The "fat clean-shaven man" believed the Intelligent Ghost's materialism would take the souls of the grey town in the wrong direction. What did he believe would be their best option to open up their "creative functions"?

9. What did the light of Heaven reveal about all the passengers? According to 1 Corinthians 3:12, how will your faith become sight when you see Christ?

CHAPTER 2 DISCUSSION NOTES:

CHAPTER 3:
SHADOW PEOPLE

The bus eventually moves beyond the dingy grey town to a new land that we soon understand to be Heaven. As the travelers arrive and exit the bus, some become overwhelmed and retreat back to the safety of the bus while others, braver, huddle together and press forward.

> *The light and coolness that drenched me were like those of summer morning, early morning a minute or two before the sunrise, only that there was a certain difference.*

Discussion Questions

1. With regards to the landscape, how does Lewis describe the passengers' new destination?

2. Using the following Bible passages, describe the nature of Heaven. In your own words, how would you describe Heaven to a friend?

   a) Matthew 6:20 –

b) Luke 23:43 –

c) John 14:2 –

d) 1 Corinthians 2:9 –

e) Hebrews 11:16 –

f) Revelation 21:1 –

g) Revelation 21:4 –

h) Revelation 22:1–5 –

i) Revelation 21:15–27 –

3. Once Lewis steps off the bus, he finds himself in a space so huge that the solar system is an "indoor affair" by comparison. It gives him a feeling of freedom but also of exposure and possible danger. Why?

4. What does Lewis fully realize about the other passengers on the bus as well as himself, and how does it affect their interaction with their surroundings?

5. Even though the bus driver said that they can stay as long as the please and never go back to the grey town, some of the Ghosts become overwhelmed with fear and retreat to the safety of the bus. Imagine how Abraham felt in Genesis 12:1 when God asked him to move his whole family without telling him where they were going. How can the fear of the unknown cripple your capacity to follow God?

6. Has God ever asked you to do something that seemed unreasonable? Something that took you into the territory of the unknown? What if He asked you to refuse a long-awaited promotion or resist a longed-for relationship? What if He called you to a remote part of the world or asked you to release your children to serve Him in a faraway place? How would you respond?

7. Why was the respectable Ghost annoyed? Which Jewish group in Luke 15:1–7 found themselves with the same complaint, and what was Jesus' response? What people groups might you feel uncomfortable with sharing your church with?

8. Lewis remarked, "There was no change and no progression as the hours passed. The promise—or the threat—of sunrise rested immovably up there." According to Matthew 25:1–13, why is there both "promise" and "threat" in the sunrise?

9. Describe the appearance of the people who came from Heaven. According to Philippians 3:20–21, how will our bodies be made different in Heaven?

CHAPTER 3 DISCUSSION NOTES:

CHAPTER 4:
I GOT MY RIGHTS

The Ghosts, completely out of their element, are now confronted with the solid people of Heaven. Lewis does not want to intrude on the heavenly conversations about to take place and moves away so as not to overhear. But the Big Man follows him, and, in turn, a Spirit follows the Big Man, so Lewis has no choice but to follow the conversation.

> *Then do. At once. Ask for the Bleeding Charity.*
> *Everything is here for the asking and nothing can be bought.*

Discussion Questions

1. Describe the appearance of the solid Spirit that approaches the Big Man. What do we learn about what sort of man he was on Earth and his relationship to the Big Man?

2. What did the Big Man find so hard to believe regarding Len? Where is Jack now?

3. The Big Man cannot accept the fact that Len can admit such a serious crime so easily and that things are "all right now." In Mark 3:28–29, for which sins did Jesus tell the Pharisees that we can be forgiven? Is there an unforgivable sin? Read Hebrews 10:26–29 and Isaiah 5:20 for further reference.

4. Death-bed confessions often bring out the self-righteous doubters who question whether those who commit heinous crimes will be allowed in Heaven upon true repentance. According to Acts 8:3, Acts 9:1, and 1 Corinthians 15:9, how would a repentant Paul, formally Saul, respond to those self-righteous doubters?

5. How does Galatians 2:20 help us understand Len's response to the Big Man's question about whether he is ashamed of himself? How does Jesus say that we should approach our past sin, in Luke 9:62?

6. What is the Big Man's concept of a decent person who should be allowed in Heaven? Why did Len not want the Big Man to continue in this line of thinking?

7. The Big Man is self-righteous and believes he is morally superior to Len. He is convinced of his own goodness and sees no reason to repent. According to 1 John 1:8–10, if we claim to be good and that we have not sinned, what do we make God out to be?

8. The murder, according to Len, is not the worst thing he ever did. What was?

9. Len does his best to persuade the Big Man to acknowledge his faults, but the Big Man wants no part of a Heaven that allows murderers to become citizens. He is only interested in getting justice or what he perceives is owed to him, not any "bleeding charity." Although this is a noble-sounding trait on Earth, what problems does it cause with getting into Heaven?

10. How does Len's invitation for the Big Man to ask for the "Bleeding Charity" and that "everything is here for the asking and nothing can be bought" parallel with Ephesians 2:8–9?

CHAPTER 4 DISCUSSION NOTES:

CHAPTER 5:
HONEST OPINIONS,
SINCERELY EXPRESSED

The fat, cultured Ghost, with whom Lewis was discussing spirituality on the bus, loves to debate—especially when it comes to spiritual matters. Upon his arrival in Heaven, he once again begins an intellectual and stimulating conversation with the Spirit sent to help him. In his pursuit for religious truth, he abandons the one truth that would allow him to stay in Heaven.

> *We were afraid of crude salvationism, afraid of a breach with the spirit of the age,*
> *afraid of ridicule, afraid (above all) of real spiritual fears and hopes.*

Discussion Questions

1. In this chapter, what more do we learn about the fat, cultured Ghost's history and his relationship to the Spirit with whom he is conversing?

2. The Ghost remembers that the Spirit had become "narrow-minded" toward the end of his earthly life, implying that the Spirit had come to believe in a literal Heaven and Hell. What is the irony in the Ghost's criticism given his current location?

3. What sort of criticisms do you see leveled at Christians today? How does Jesus tell us to respond in Matthew 5:11–12 when we are insulted for our faith?

4. According to the Spirit, what is the fat, cultured Ghost's sin? What sort of people or personalities might you consider to be an apostate today?

5. In Jude 3–4, Jude outlines how to recognize apostasy and strongly urges those in the body of Christ to contend earnestly for the faith. The Greek word translated "contend earnestly" is a compound verb from which we get the word "agonize." What sort of description is Jude portraying in our battle for biblical truth? Who is called to this battle— just church leaders?

6. The Ghost thinks his formed opinions were not only honest but heroic and risky, and he did not understand why he should be penalized for expressing them. Why did the Spirit tell him that his opinions were neither heroic nor risky? Did they really risk anything, or rather, did they gain from their opinions?

7. At one point, with unusual intensity, the Spirit tells the Ghost, "We are not playing now." Why did he use this approach here? Why is Paul so adamant in Romans 13:11 that it's time to wake up from your spiritual slumber? Have you ever used this direct of an approach with a friend or family member?

8. The Spirit asks the Episcopal Ghost a very pivotal question: "You have seen Hell: you are in sight of Heaven. Will you, even now, repent and believe?" What parallel question does Jesus ask in Matthew 16:15 and John 11:26, and why is this an important question for everyone?

9. The Ghost seems remotely interested in following his Spirit guide if he can be given certain assurances that his talents will be used in Heaven. How does the Spirit respond to this request? How do you feel about the fact that along with your unworthiness of Heaven, you are also not needed, according to Lewis?

10. The great tragedy here is the Ghost's inability to grasp that there are such things as fact, truth, and Christ. Not able to break away from his desire, what does the Ghost remember that it must do that is more important than going to Heaven?

CHAPTER 5 DISCUSSION NOTES:

CHAPTER 6:
DIVINE WATERFALL AND HEAVY APPLES

As Lewis continues to explore his heavenly surrounding, he finds that his senses have been altered from what they were in the grey town or on Earth. We also gain further insight into the difficulty of trying to steal from Heaven.

> *On Earth, such a waterfall could not have been perceived at all as a whole; it was too big. Its sound would have been a terror in the woods for twenty miles.*

Discussion Questions

1. What more does Lewis continue to experience and learn about his current form and his senses as he explores Heaven?

2. What Ghost does he see sneaking through the trees around the waterfall? From our previous study in Chapter 2, what do we know about this Ghost and his plan?

3. What specifically was Ikey trying to steal, and what problems did he encounter while doing so?

4. Note the capital "T" on tree that Ikey was attempting to steal from. Read Genesis 2:9, Genesis 3:24, and Revelation 2:7. What significance might there be in this "Tree"? Why do you think God has limited our lifespan and barred us from a tree that can provide eternal life in this world?

5. Who stops Ikey from trying to sneak back to the bus with an apple, and why can he not take it with him?

6. The Angel calls Ikey a fool for his efforts. The Hebrew word for fool is "nabal," meaning an irreverent person who has no perception of ethical or religious truth—senseless. It does not refer to intelligence. According to Psalm 14:1, he or she is a fool if they claim there is no God. Using John 3:16 and Matthew 28:19–20 as guides, how should Christians treat those "fools" who claim there is no God?

7. The Greek word Jesus used for fool is "aphrōn," and it means "without reason" or "senseless." Using this definition, why did Jesus refer to the man in Luke 12:16–21 as a fool?

8. Read Proverbs 26:11. Why did the Angel refer to Ikey as a fool?

9. What was the Angel's solution to Ikey's desire for an apple? Did he take the Angel up on his suggestion?

10. The character of Ikey illustrates the pathetic nature of greed and selfishness. He is willing to undergo severe pain and suffering just so he can try to make a profit in Hell even when what is being offered to him is so much more fulfilling. He can have an abundance of apples if he just stays. How does 1 Timothy 6:10 further describe Ikey's struggle with greed?

CHAPTER 6 DISCUSSION NOTES:

CHAPTER 7:
THE HARD-BITTEN GHOST

Up to this point, Lewis has been listening in to the various dialogs between Ghosts and Spirits. Now he will have a very discouraging conversation with a hard-bitten Ghost.

> *They lead you to expect red fire and devils and all sorts of*
> *interesting people sizzling on grids—Henry VIII and all that—*
> *but when you get there it's just like any other town.*

Discussion Questions

1. How would you define the term "hard-bitten"? How does Lewis initially describe the Hard-Bitten Ghost?

2. Because the Ghost had become cynical in his earthly life, what sort of conspiracy theories had he developed? What sort of conspiracy theories has he now started to develop about Heaven and Hell?

3. How can a cynical mindset—an inclination to believe that other people are motivated purely by self-interest—be dangerous in our relationships, views on faith, and general outlook on life?

4. Cynicism is in fact a form of self-righteousness in that the cynic always knows a better way. Read Psalm 1:1. What tends to make you cynical in life and perhaps join in with a group of mockers?

5. According to Ephesians 4:31–32, how does the Bible teach us to deal with cynicism and bitterness?

6. The Hard-Bitten Ghost laments that if Heaven and Hell were really at war, Heaven could overrun Hell and rescue its inhabitants. Read Leviticus 26:13, Psalm 107:19, Acts 16:31, Galatians 1:3–4, and Hebrews 7:25. In both the Old and New Testaments, how do we see God constantly rescuing His people?

7. When asked what he would choose, Heaven or Hell, the Hard-Bitten Ghost becomes indignant and says, "They keep on asking us to alter ourselves. But if the people who run the show are so clever and so powerful, why don't they find something to suit the public?" In other words, he did not think that he should have to change but rather Heaven should adapt to him. Read Ephesians 4:22–24 and Romans 12:2. What type of change is required to truly embrace our lives as born-again believers?

8. The Hard-Bitten Ghost has given up on happiness so that when the ultimate happiness, paradise in Heaven, is finally presented to him, he cannot accept it. C.S. Lewis writes in *Mere Christianity*, "If we find ourselves with a desire that nothing in this world can satisfy, the most probable explanation is that we were made for another world." How will constantly striving for happiness leave one cynical like the Hard-Bitten Ghost, who thinks any happiness he finds is going to be a fraud anyway? Read Psalm 144:15 and Proverbs 3:13. How should a Christian view happiness?

CHAPTER 7 DISCUSSION NOTES:

CHAPTER 8:
GHOSTLY VANITY

After his miserable conversation with the Hard-Bitten Ghost, Lewis begins to doubt Heaven and the good intentions of those who are there. This induces him to fear and nearly causes him to return to the grey town. Then he overhears a discussion between a bright person and a very self-conscious Ghost.

> *Shame is like that. If you will accept it—if you will drink the cup to the bottom—you will find it very nourishing: but try to do anything else with it and it scalds.*

Discussion Questions

1. As Lewis reflects on his conversation with the Hard-Bitten Ghost, he begins to question the essential goodness of the bright spirits and why they do not take more action to help the people in Hell. Do you think it's ever wrong to question God? Why or why not?

2. Lewis begins to confront his fear and considers whether Heaven might be a very dangerous place for him. In. C.S. Lewis's *The Lion, the Witch, and the Wardrobe*, Susan confronts her fear about meeting Aslan the Lion and asks, "Is he quite safe?" Mr. Beaver responds with, "Who said anything about safe? Course he isn't safe. But he's good." Read the passages below and note the danger that comes from interacting with God and following Jesus.

    a) Matthew 10:34–36 –

    b) Mark 1:18 –

    c) Romans 12:1–2 –

    d) Matthew 6:19–21 –

    e) Matthew 28:19–20 –

3. Describe the Well-Dressed Ghost and what her main issues are with the Bright Spirit who approaches her.

4. God never uses one's outward physical appearance to determine beauty or worth. In 1 Samuel 16:7, what did God instruct the prophet Samuel to examine when searching for the next king of

5. In 1 Peter 3:3–4, what does Peter direct Christian women to focus on? How difficult do you think this is in today's culture?

6. Why is transparency with God over our sin and shame so important for us to ever experience genuine repentance and God's grace?

7. The Spirit urges the woman to not be afraid to be seen, flaws and all, and that none of it will matter if she will only exercise her faith. If we believe Psalm 139:14, why is it important that we embrace who we are, flaws and all, in order to exercise our faith?

8. How do you interpret the Spirit's invitation to the Ghost when he said, "To the mountains—you need to go. You can lean on me all the way. I can't absolutely carry you, but you need have almost no weight on your own feet: and it will hurt less at every step"? Read 2 Corinthians 1:5 and Isaiah 41:10 for further reference.

9. Although we are left to wonder, why do you think the Spirit calls the herd of unicorns, and what would be the hopeful outcome of this encounter?

CHAPTER 8 DISCUSSION NOTES:

CHAPTER 9:
QUESTIONS AND ANSWERS

After witnessing a variety of conversations and actions between Ghosts and Spirits, Lewis is confused, miserable, and somewhat fearful. Then, at last, he is approached by his guiding spirit, who is none other than author, poet, and Christian minister George MacDonald.

> *There are only two kinds of people in the end: those who say to God, "Thy will be done," and those to whom God says, in the end, "Thy will be done."*

Discussion Questions

1. Lewis begins to gush when he unexpectedly encounters his earthly "hero," George MacDonald. MacDonald stops Lewis, assuring him that he knows all about his admiration and past, even noting that his "memory misleads you in one or two particulars." What earthly "hero" would you lavish with praise if you met them in Heaven and why?

2. MacDonald persuades Lewis to continue on with his questions about this place he finds himself in. What are Lewis's questions?

3. What is the Refrigerium? It appears as though the ghosts from Hell take these excursions all the time. What other destinations do they choose?

4. Lewis asks MacDonald, "Is judgement not final? Is there really a way out of Hell into Heaven?" What is MacDonald's reply to whether or not our eternal destination is determined before death?

5. The story seems to suggest that we have a real choice after death—that there is salvation for the dead. Read John 5:28–29. What is a Christian's response as to whether or not our eternal destination is determined before death? What options did the rich man have in Hell in Luke 16:19–31?

6. Why is it comforting to hope "that heaven, once attained, works backwards and will turn even that agony into a glory" or, in other words, that all of your past troubles will now be set in context?

7. Regarding those who reject eternal life with God, MacDonald says, "The choice of every lost soul can be expressed in the words 'Better to reign in Hell than serve in Heaven.'" According to John 3:19–21, why do people ultimately reject God? How can you determine whether a person's intellectual objections are genuine or just a smokescreen to hide the fact that they love their sin?

8. MacDonald gives another example of a scientist whose research consumed his life and who eventually died and made it to the "Valley of the Shadow of Life." He did not continue on to the mountains because there was nothing there to prove, no question that he could provide an answer for. Had he been able to overcome this disappointment, he could have begun again as "a little child and entered into joy." Jesus reinforces this idea in Matthew 18:13 and Mark 10:15. Why are little children the perfect model for how we are to come to Christ?

9. Recalling his conversation with the Hard-Bitten Ghost, what is MacDonald's answer to Lewis's question as to why the solid people, since they are full of love, don't venture to Hell to rescue the Ghosts?

10. Lewis's next concern is for all the poor Ghosts who never make it to the bus stop. MacDonald responds by defining two types of people. Who are they?

11. MacDonald provides further clarification on the Ghosts who do not make it to the bus stop when he says, "All that are in Hell, choose it." Do you believe that those who end up in Hell actually choose it over Heaven? Using the following verses, summarize how man's free will and God's sovereignty work together in salvation.

    a) Romans 8:29 and John 15:16 – Who determines who is saved?

    b) Romans 5:16 – Who takes the first step in salvation?

    c) John 3:16, John 12:32, Romans 10:13, and Titus 2:11 – Who is salvation made available to?

    d) Romans 10:9–10 – What must man do to be saved?

    e) 2 Corinthians 5:17 – What is the result of our salvation?

12. What is Lewis's concern about the Grumbling Ghost? What was MacDonald's response to his concerns and the dangers of grumbling? Do you think MacDonald is too severe in his judgment of grumbling?

13. Describe the other types of Ghosts that come near to Heaven but do not stay.

   a) Teaching Ghost –

   b) Tub-Thumping Ghosts –

   c) Planning Ghosts –

   d) Materialist Ghosts: –

   e) Bogie Ghosts –

14. Regarding these Ghosts who appear to be vile and unredeemable, Lewis wonders why they are even here to begin with. What is MacDonald's response? Do you think there is some truth in his explanation? Why or why not?

15. The Artist Ghost was quite famous on Earth and had begun painting as a means to tell about the light. Over time, he lost that desire and just painted for painting's sake. What does Revelation 2:4–5 tell us about rekindling that passion we had for Jesus when we first became Christians?

16. From this conversation, we learn that if Ghosts continue on their destination into Heaven, they will encounter a fountain. What is the result of their drinking from this fountain? According to Ephesians 2:8–9 and Isaiah 64:6, what should be our approach to the works we accomplish here on Earth?

17. The Ghost, with little enthusiasm, begins his walk with the Spirit, believing that at least there will be interesting people to meet in Heaven and that his life's works will be enjoyed in posterity by those on Earth. What contradictory information does he learn that causes him to abandon the trip to Heaven?

CHAPTER 9 DISCUSSION NOTES:

CHAPTER 10:
SELFLESS OR SELFISH

Lewis overhears the conversation of a Female Ghost who on Earth was a very frustrated wife devoted to advancing her husband's career and shaping his life. She demands and then finally pleads with Hilda, one of the Bright People, to return her husband to her so that she might continue her selfish endeavor to control him in the afterlife.

> *Give him back to me. Why should he have everything his own way? It's not good for him. It isn't right, it's not fair. I want Robert. What right have you to keep him from me? I hate you. How can I pay him out if you won't let me have him?*

Discussion Questions

1. How would you describe the Female Ghost? How would you describe her husband, Robert?

2. The Female Ghost says she can forgive her husband but she cannot forget. Do you believe as Christians we are called to both forgive and forget? Can we truly forget that which is done to us? How should we approach a situation where the offender does not desire forgiveness? Use the following verses as guides: Matthew 6:14, Ephesians 4:32, Hebrews 8:12, Philippians 3:13, and Matthew 10:16.

3. The Female Ghost carries out her agenda of manipulating her husband with all the appearances of selflessness and love. First Corinthians 13:4–8 is often recited at weddings as a pattern for an ideal marriage. Provide an example of how the wife violated each one of Paul's descriptions about love.

   a) Love is patient –

   b) Love is kind –

   c) Love does not envy or boast –

   d) Love does not dishonor others –

   e) Love is not self-seeking –

   f) Love is not easily angered –

   g) Love does not keep a record of wrongs –

   h) Love does not delight in evil –

4. What does it mean that "Love always protects, always trusts, always hopes, always perseveres. Love never fails"?

5. The Female Ghost's own self-image is validated through her husband's success. She has not learned to love God or herself and therefore cannot love her husband properly. Read Matthew 22:36–39. What are some examples of self-hate, and how does this render us less capable of following Christ?

6. The Female Ghost claims that she only wants what's best for Robert. However, no matter how far she pushes him, he never seems to "arrive." Why is this? How can this be a dangerous trap, particularly when parenting children?

7. What is the Female Ghost's offer to Hilda, the Bright Ghost, regarding Robert?

8. How does the absence of Hilda's defense of Robert turn out to be his best defense? What does the Female Ghost eventually reveal about her motives?

CHAPTER 10 DISCUSSION NOTES:

CHAPTER 11:
LOVE AND LIZARDS

The next conversation Lewis and MacDonald witness is a Bright Spirit conversing with a Motherly Ghost who struggles with bitterness over her son's death. This is immediately followed by a magnificent encounter between an Angel, an Oily Ghost, and a lizard.

> *No natural feelings are high or low, holy or unholy, in themselves. They are all holy when God's hand is on the rein. They all go bad when they set up on their own and make themselves into false gods.*

Discussion Questions

1. Describe the circumstances surrounding the encounter between Pam, the Motherly Ghost, and her brother, Reginald, the Bright Spirit. What prevents the Motherly Ghost from growing solid? What must she learn to do if she wants to see her son, Michael?

2. Pam irritably claims that she'll love God as long as this brings her back to Michael, but Reginald points out that this way of thinking is no good. Loving God cannot be a means to an end of reuniting with Michael. Have you ever had a friend, family member, or colleague who only desired your friendship for as long as you had something to give them? What reasons might people have for behaving this way before God? How does Jesus support what it means to "want God for His own sake" in John 6:26–27?

3. What was Reginald's answer to Pam's question about why, if God loved her, did He take Michael away from her? How did Pam's motherly love violate God's command in Exodus 20:1–6?

4. Pam's obsession with her son allows her grief to consume her even to the extent of keeping his room the same, ignoring the rest of her family, and choosing to live in the past and not letting go. Have you witnessed examples of this in your own life or in the lives of others? How can grief, if taken to extremes, impact our relationships with other people?

5. Pam thinks Reginald is upset because she did not love either him or their mother as she should have. Reginald responds with "Don't you know that you can't hurt anyone in this country?" Read 1 Corinthians 15:54–57 and Philippians 1:21. How does the fact that there is no "sting" or "hurt" in death impact the way we live on this earth and our expectations of Heaven?

6. As MacDonald and Lewis move away from the siblings' conversation, MacDonald recites Luke 18:19 when he says, "There is but one good; that is God. Everything else is good when it looks to Him and bad when it turns from Him." How can the "good" feelings of motherly love, sexual love, tolerance, patriotism, work ethic, commitment, family, intellect, etc., be corrupted and become "bad feelings"?

7. Describe the Dark and Oily Ghost and his pet. What do we later learn that the lizard is a symbol for?

8. As this Ghost begins to head back to the bus, he is approached by not just a Spirit guide but an Angel emitting light and heat at the same time. What offer does the Angel make to the Ghost, and what must the Ghost do to receive the offer? According to Matthew 7:7, Luke 11:13, and John 14:14, what is an essential component in the interaction between God and His Angels and the human race?

9. List all the reasons the ghost gives for not being ready to give permission for the lizard to be killed?

10. The Angel explains that all time is captured here and now in Heaven and that the gradual approach or to delay killing the lizard will not work. When removing sin from our lives, why does the gradual approach not work?

11. The Angel assures the Ghost that killing the lizard will not kill the Ghost, but what about any pain the Ghost might experience? The ancient method of washing clothes was by beating or treading. With that illustration, how do you interpret David's request to God to cleanse him of sin in Psalm 51:7? Read Matthew 18:7–9. How seriously should we approach removing sin?

12. The Ghost complains that the Angel could have just killed the lizard before he knew all these new details and it would have already been over with. Why didn't the Angel just do that? Why doesn't God just remove our struggles when we become Christians? Read 2 Corinthians 12:7.

13. Why do we as Christians, who know right from wrong, continue to keep lust or any "pet sin"? How does Paul describe his frustration of dealing with sin in Romans 7:14–20? What is Paul's conclusion in Romans 7:24–25?

14. The lizard, sensing danger, begins to whisper again about how the Angel can indeed kill him, and what would the Ghost be then? How can we guard ourselves from being deceived by our own sin delusions? Read Hebrews 3:13.

15. Finally, the Ghost realizes it would be better to be dead than to live with this creature. What did the Angel do next? What type of repentance from the Ghost do we see is this passage? Regardless of our sin, according to Romans 10:13, who can call out for salvation? What does 2 Corinthians 3:18 state will happen once we do?

CHAPTER 11 DISCUSSION NOTES:

CHAPTER 12:
SARAH, FRANK, AND
THE TRAGEDIAN

Lewis and MacDonald come across an angelic procession honoring a Heavenly woman named Sarah Smith, who evidently saved many souls while she was on Earth. While this saintly Spirit is passing through the woods. she encounters a Ghost. who was her earthly husband.

> *Few men looked on her without becoming, in a certain fashion, her lovers. But it was the kind of love that made them not less true, but truer, to their own wives.*

Discussion Questions

1. What do we know about Sarah Smith? Who do you think Lewis most likely mistakes her for?

2. Why does Lewis choose an ordinary name like "Sarah Smith" for this saintly Spirit? Using Matthew 19:29–30 as a guide, what does MacDonald mean when he says, "Fame in the country and fame on Earth are two quite different things"? Does our earthly rank automatically translate into an inverse heavenly rank?

3. Sarah is confronted by her earthly husband, a dwarf named Frank, who pulls a tragedian—an old-school, melodramatic actor who specializes in tragic roles—by a chain. How would you describe Frank's earthly character as it relates to his wife, Sarah? What question is he most concerned with asking her in the afterlife?

4. What is the relationship between Frank and the Tragedian? What is it so hard for Frank to be free from the Tragedian?

5. The Tragedian persona was created by Frank's desire to make others feel guilty and then extract pleasure from their guilt. Why do people create alter egos or new personas to define them? What are the dangers of continuing to act out that persona around others, and how hard is it to give up?

6. What do Galatians 2:20 and 2 Corinthians 5:17 teach us about our nature or "persona" as a new believer in Christ? What about our "old self" disappears, and what takes its place? How is Christianity different than other personas we could take on?

7. Early in the chapter, Sarah's very first action is to ask for Frank's forgiveness. What do we later learn she is asking forgiveness from? How does Frank take this news?

8. Sarah notes that she now knows what love is because she is truly "IN love" or in the presence of God's love. According to 1 John 4:8, what is an accurate description for God? How is perfect love described in 1 Corinthians 13:4–8? How difficult is it for you to embody these character traits all the time?

9. Sarah smiles beautifully and explains that in the afterlife, there is no such thing as need—and as a result, she and Frank can truly love one another. Heaven seems to be a place where there are no longer any "needs." How will we know what to do? How to function? What will we pursue? Will it matter? Read Revelation 7:16–17.

10. The Tragedian overreacts to this news, claiming that he wishes Sarah were dead at his feet. In response, Sarah laughs and counsels him to rid himself of the Tragedian, who is speaking for him with a dramatic yet self-destructive attitude. How does Frank respond to her laughing? How can laughter, like fear, help someone step outside of themselves and see matters from a different angle?

CHAPTER 12 DISCUSSION NOTES:

CHAPTER 13:
ONE LAST SHOT AT JOY

As Sarah continues to address Frank's desire to make her feel miserable despite the joy around him, Lewis questions MacDonald about how the blessed in Heaven can be happy if they know that their loved ones are in Hell, cut off from the very happiness they enjoy.

> *All Hell is smaller than one pebble of your earthly world; but it is smaller than one atom of this world, the Real World.*

Discussion Questions

1. As Frank tries to keep from laughing along with Sarah, he becomes aware of the absurdity of the Tragedian. Even so, Frank jerks the chain and begins screaming, "You dare to laugh at it!" and blames Sarah for his going back to Hell. What is Sarah's response? Do you think it is possible for Frank to experience true joy? What would be required?

2. Read James 1:2–4. How is it possible to experience joy in the midst of a painful or difficult situation? What about through bankruptcy, cancer, or even losing a child? How can both joy and pain exist together?

3. Read the following scripture passages about joy, and then answer the following questions.

   a) 1 Thessalonians 1:6 – Where does our joy come from?

   b) 1 Thessalonians 5:16-18 – What is the difference in giving thanks "for" our circumstances and giving thanks "in" our circumstances?

   c) Hebrews 10:34 – Why did those is this passage accept their suffering and have joy?

   d) Hebrews 12:2 – Why did Jesus endure the shame and scorn of the cross?

4. Sarah begs Frank to stop using pity in the wrong way and offers him love and kindness and the opportunity for true joy—but not pity. Read Psalm 72:13 and Luke 10:33. When can pity be an appropriate emotion to show? How is pity different from feeling sorry for someone? When can it become a dangerous weapon?

5. Determined to be joyless, Frank is consumed by the Tragedian, who vanishes in Sarah's bright presence. As Sarah leaves, Lewis asks how Sarah can be untouched by Frank's damnation. What is MacDonald's response? How do you think you would respond watching a loved one choose Hell over Heaven?

6. Lewis wonders aloud why Sarah didn't go down to Hell to visit Frank—she could have at least gone to the bus stop to see him off. What is MacDonald's reply as to why the Bright Spirits don't pursue their loved ones to the bus stop or even all the way into Hell? How does this enhance your perception of the expansiveness of Heaven?

7. It seems as though, outside of some supernatural expansion, Hell is so small that it cannot be gotten into. MacDonald did say that only One had the power to make Himself small enough to descend into Hell. Read 1 Peter 3:18–20 and Ephesians 4:8–10. Do you think Jesus spent the Saturday after His death preaching in Hell? What other plausible explanations might there be?

8. MacDonald says, "…all loneliness, angers, hatreds, envies and itchings that it contains, if rolled into one single experience and put into the scale against the least moment of the joy that is felt by the least in Heaven, would have no weight that could be registered at all." How does this shape your perspective on the evil and suffering we experience in this world?

9. MacDonald seems to be emphasizing humanity's "free will" (the belief that man's own choice impacts his destiny) over "universalism" (the belief that all will be saved in the end) and "predestination" (the belief that God has planned man's ultimate fate). God is omnipotent, so He "knows" what we are about to do because to Him, we already did it. There is no before or during or after "time" for Him. How does the fact that God sees all points in time impact your understanding of your free will and God's sovereignty?

CHAPTER 13 DISCUSSION NOTES:

CHAPTER 14:
THE CHESS GAME

MacDonald responds to Lewis's question about the ultimate fate of humanity by showing him a huge chessboard symbolizing the structure of the universe.

> *Do not ask of a vision in a dream more than a vision in a dream can give.*

Discussion Questions

1. Lewis finds himself in the midst of a "great assembly of gigantic forms" all surrounding a silver table with little figures on it like chessmen moving about. Who did the giants, chessman, and table represent? What are the Giants doing? What is the purpose of "Time" within the context of the chessboard?

2. Based on what Lewis sees, he questions whether humans are actually free to make choices or if everything is predetermined in the same sense that a chess piece's moves can be planned in advance. What is MacDonald's response?

3. MacDonald then reveals to Lewis that he has been dreaming the entire time. Why does MacDonald instruct Lewis to make it very clear to other people that his vision of the afterlife was just a dream—not the truth about the afterlife?

4. Why is Lewis both surprised and terrified when the sun begins to rise high in the east and he hears voices singing, "Sleepers awake!"? What is his sense of urgency?

5. Using Ephesians 5:13–16 as a reference, what is the significance of the sunrise from both a literary (the story) and spiritual perspective?

6. What similarities do you notice between Lewis's real word and the grey town?

CHAPTER 14 DISCUSSION NOTES:

Quotes

All of C.S. Lewis's writings are extremely quotable. In fact, if you search the web, you will find plenty of them, including websites, Facebook pages, and Twitter feeds dedicated to the task. On the next several pages, you will find some of my favorite quotes from *The Great Divorce*. I'm sure you have your own!

PREFACE

A sum can be put right: but only by going back till you find the error and working it afresh from that point, never by simply going on.

I think earth, if chosen instead of Heaven, will turn out to have been, all along, only a region in Hell: and earth, if put second to Heaven, to have been from the beginning a part of Heaven itself.

If we insist on keeping Hell (or even Earth) we shall not see Heaven: if we accept Heaven we shall not be able to retain even the smallest and most intimate souvenirs of Hell.

I do not think that all who choose wrong roads perish; but their rescue consists in being put back on the right road. A sum can be put right: but only by going back til you find the error and working it afresh from that point, never by simply going on. Evil can be undone, but it cannot "develop" into good. Time does not heal it. The spell must be unwound, bit by bit, "with backward mutters of dissevering power"—or else not.

I believe, to be sure, that any man who reaches Heaven will find that what he abandoned (even in plucking out his right eye) has not been lost: that the kernel of what he was really seeking even in his most depraved wishes will be there, beyond expectation, waiting for him in "the High Countries".

CHAPTER 1

Why on earth they insist on coming I can't imagine. They won't like it at all when we get there, and they'd really be much more comfortable at home.

CHAPTER 2

The trouble is they have no Needs. You get everything you want (not very good quality, of course) by just imagining it.

CHAPTER 3

The light and coolness that drenched me were like those of summer morning, early morning a minute or two before the sunrise, only that there was a certain difference.

The promise—or the threat—of sunrise rested immovably up there.

CHAPTER 4

I only want my rights. I'm not asking for anybody's bleeding charity.

Then do. At once. Ask for the Bleeding Charity. Everything is here for the asking and nothing can be bought.

CHAPTER 5

Do you really think there are no sins of intellect?

When, in our whole lives, did we honestly face, in solitude, the one question on which all turned: whether after all the Supernatural might not in fact occur? When did we put up one moment's real resistance to the loss of our faith?

We were afraid of crude salvationism, afraid of a breach with the spirit of the age, afraid of ridicule, afraid (above all) of real spiritual fears and hopes.

You have seen Hell: you are in sight of Heaven. Will you, even now, repent and believe?

We know nothing of religion here: we only think of Christ.

You can begin as if nothing had ever gone wrong. White as snow.

CHAPTER 6

On Earth, such a waterfall could not have been perceived at all as a whole; it was too big. Its sound would have been a terror in the woods for twenty miles.

CHAPTER 7

They lead you to expect red fire and devils and all sorts of interesting people sizzling on grids— Henry VIII and all that—but when you get there it's just like any other town.

CHAPTER 8

Shame is like that. If you will accept it—if you will drink the cup to the bottom—you will find it very nourishing: but try to do anything else with it and it scalds.

CHAPTER 9

There are only two kinds of people in the end: those who say to God, "Thy will be done," and those to whom God says, in the end, "Thy will be done."

Those that hate goodness are sometimes nearer than those that know nothing at all about it and think they have it.

There have been men before…who got so interested in proving the existence of God that they came to care nothing for God himself…as if the good Lord had nothing to do but to exist.

The sane would do no good if they made themselves mad to help madmen.

They say of some temporal suffering, "No future bliss can make up for it" not knowing that Heaven, once attained, will work backwards and turn even that agony into a glory.

The choice of every lost soul can be expressed in the words "Better to reign in Hell than serve in Heaven."

No soul that seriously and constantly desires joy will ever miss it. Those who seek find. To those who knock it is opened.

CHAPTER 10

Give him back to me. Why should he have everything his own way? It's not good for him. It isn't right, it's not fair. I want Robert. What right have you to keep him from me? I hate you. How can I pay him out if you won't let me have him?

CHAPTER 11

There is no other day. All days are present now. This moment contains all moments.

There is but one good; that is God. Everything else is good when it looks to Him and bad when it turns from Him.

You cannot love a fellow creature fully till you love God.

No natural feelings are high or low, holy or unholy, in themselves. They are all holy when God's hand is on the rein. They all go bad when they set up on their own and make themselves into false gods.

Every natural love will rise again and live forever in this country: but none will rise again until it has been buried.

Lust is a poor, weak, whimpering, whispering thing compared with that richness and energy of desire which will arise when lust has been killed.

CHAPTER 12

Few men looked on her without becoming, in a certain fashion, her lovers. But it was the kind of love that made them not less true, but truer, to their own wives.

CHAPTER 13

And yet all loneliness, angers, hatreds, envies, and itchings that [Hell] contains, if rolled into one single experience and put into the scale against the least moment of the joy that is felt by the least in Heaven, would have no weight that could be registered at all.

Good beats upon the damned incessantly as sound waves beat on the ears of the deaf, but they cannot receive it. Their fists are clenched, their teeth are clenched, their eyes fast shut. First they will not, in the end they cannot, open their hands for gifts, or their mouth for food, or their eyes to see.

All Hell is smaller than one pebble of your earthly world; but it is smaller than one atom of this world, the Real World.

That thing is Freedom: the gift whereby ye most resemble your Maker and are yourselves part of eternal reality.

A sum can be put right: but only by going back till you find the error and working it afresh from that point, never by simply going on.

CHAPTER 14

Do not ask of a vision in a dream more than a vision in a dream can give.

MERE CHRISTIANITY STUDY GUIDE

A Bible Study on the C.S. Lewis Book *Mere Christianity*

By Steven Urban

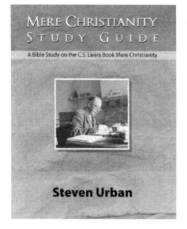

Mere Christianity Study Guide takes participants through a study of C.S. Lewis's classic *Mere Christianity*. Yet despite its recognition as a "classic," there is surprisingly little available today in terms of a serious study course.

This 12-week Bible study digs deep into each chapter and, in turn, into Lewis's thoughts. Perfect for small group sessions, this interactive workbook includes daily, individual study as well as a complete appendix and commentary to supplement and further clarify certain topics. Multiple week format options are also included.

WHAT OTHERS ARE SAYING:

This study guide is more than just a guide to C.S Lewis' Mere Christianity, it is a guide to Christianity itself. – Crystal

Wow! What a lot of insight and food for thought! Perfect supplement to Mere Christianity. I think Mr. Lewis himself would approve. – Laurie

Our group is in the middle of studying Mere Christianity and I have found this guide to be invaluable. – Angela

This is a very useful and comprehensive guide to Mere Christianity. – John

To learn more about Mere Christianity Study Guide or to find retailers please visit
www.BrownChairBooks.com

THE SCREWTAPE LETTERS STUDY GUIDE

A Bible Study on the C.S. Lewis Book *The Screwtape Letters*

By Alan Vermilye

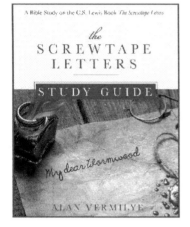

The Screwtape Letters Study Guide takes participants through a study of C.S. Lewis's classic, *The Screwtape Letters*.

This Bible study digs deep into each letter from Screwtape, an undersecretary in the lowerarchy of Hell, to his incompetent nephew Wormwood a junior devil. Perfect for small group sessions this interactive workbook includes daily, individual study with a complete answer guide available online.

Designed as a 12-week study, multiple week format options are also included.

WHAT OTHERS ARE SAYING:

This book and study creates a positive reinforcement on fighting that Spiritual battle in life. Great read, great study guide! – Lester

This study guide was a wonderful way for our group to work through the Screwtape Letters! - Becky

Use this Study Guide for a Fresh "Seeing" of the Screwtape Letters! – William

This is an essential companion if you are reading The Screwtape Letters as a small group. – J.T.

To learn more about The Screwtape Letters Study Guide or to find retailers please visit
www.BrownChairBooks.com

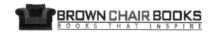

THE SCREWTAPE LETTERS STUDY GUIDE FOR TEENS

A Bible Study for Teenagers on the C.S. Lewis Book *The Screwtape Letters*

By Alan Vermilye

The Screwtape Letters Study Guide for Teens takes teenagers through a study of the C.S. Lewis classic, *The Screwtape Letters*.

Created specifically for teenagers, each daily study is designed to take them through each letter written by Screwtape, an undersecretary in the lowerarchy of Hell, to his incompetent nephew Wormwood, a junior devil.

The interactive workbook is perfect for individual study or group study to include youth groups, homeschool groups, or small groups.

SCREWTAPE PROPOSES A TOAST STUDY GUIDE

A Bible Study on the C.S. Lewis Essay *Screwtape Proposes a Toast*

By Alan Vermilye

Only the imaginative mind of C.S. Lewis could create a short story about a demon offering the after-dinner speech at the graduation ceremony at the Tempters' Training College for young demons.

Nearly two decades after the release of *The Screwtape Letters* and to the delight of his fans, Lewis wrote a sequel that he never intended to create. In fact, he never imagined the original book would become a classic and that his readers would continue to enjoy it so many years later.

Screwtape Proposes a Toast Study Guide digs deep into this classic and provides a Bible study for individual use or small groups. This flexible study can be used in one long setting or divided up over several sessions.

To learn more about either of these books or to find retailers please visit
www.BrownChairBooks.com

THE 90-DAY BIBLE STUDY GUIDE

A Bible Study Tour of the Greatest Story Ever Told

By Bruce Gust

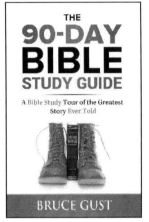

The 90-Day Bible Study Guide takes you on a journey through select portions of Scripture covering a survey of the Bible in just 90 days! The perfect Bible study for beginners, bible study for teens, homeschool groups, adult Bible studies, or those seasoned veterans looking for a refresher Bible study course.

Beginning with Genesis and ending in Revelations, you'll spend just under 30 minutes each day in this Bible Study Guide and workbook on Scripture readings and corresponding Bible study questions designed to guide you to a better understanding of the personalities, the history, the conflicts, the miracles and the Truth that is the Christian faith.

WHAT OTHERS ARE SAYING:

Bruce Gust takes us back to the basics with easy to digest truths and thought provoking questions!
– Russell

This study guide seeks to challenge you to find out the truth from God's word by reading the Bible.
- Stephen

A great way to dig into various parts of Scripture, all the while getting a bigger picture of the overall Story of the Bible. - Allie

Simple, informative and it highlights the main storyline in the Bible, redemption. Well done! – Jim

To learn more about The 90-Day Bible Study Guide or to find retailers please visit
www.BrownChairBooks.com

24995704R00062

Made in the USA
San Bernardino, CA
08 February 2019